My name is Gaylord 'Gabe' Kemling. I was a licensed Wisconsin private detective; or called a Wisconsin private eye. I worked for and with Steve Brickman who owned a detective agency that was licensed in Wisconsin for years. The agency shut down in March of 2016 when Steve Brickman passed away. His death was very hard on me.

During the partnership of doing investigations over the years, Steve and I occasionally, after a day's work was done, would sit down and write about that day's investigation work, if it was worth writing about. We could complete the story, type it out, edit it and then preserve the story for future use. We usually did all this work throughout the night, but sometimes would wait until the next morning.

These are real detective stories that Steve and I worked together on over the years. When at times we met the good, bad, and the ugly.

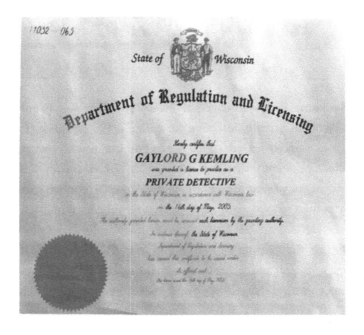

State of Wisconsin

Department of Regulation and Licensing

Hereby certifies that

GAYLORD G KEMLING

was granted a license to practice as a

PRIVATE DETECTIVE

in the State of Wisconsin in accordance with Wisconsin law

on the 16th day of May, 2005.

These are real life stories that took place in the life of a private detective in the state of Wisconsin, and other states, in the past fifteen years, 2005 to 2020. I have enclosed a collection of twelve stories from my many years as a private detective.

In Loving Memory of
Steven Thomas Brinkman

October 15, 1967 to March 7, 2016

Steven Brinkman was a very big, strong man. A great detective and a very good friend. We did a lot of work together over the years. It's hard to lose a good friend.

Gabe G. Kemling

Gabe Kemling

A DETECTIVE FROM SMALL TOWN AMERICA

True Detective Stories

AUSTIN MACAULEY PUBLISHERS™

LONDON • CAMBRIDGE • NEW YORK • SHARJAH

Ordering Information
Quantity sales: Special discounts are available on quantity purchases by corporations, associations, and others. For details, contact the publisher at the address below.

Publisher's Cataloging-in-Publication data
Kemling, Gabe
A Detective from Small Town America

ISBN 9781649791436 (Paperback)
ISBN 9781649791443 (ePub e-book)

Library of Congress Control Number: 2021916392

www.austinmacauley.com/us

First Published 2022
Austin Macauley Publishers LLC
40 Wall Street, 33rd Floor, Suite 3302
New York, NY 10005
USA

mail-usa@austinmacauley.com
+1 (646) 5125767

Table of Contents

Grandma on the Run

The Set Up

Opened up today's mail. Got a new assignment: Serve an old lady divorce papers. My client's cover letter told me she was a 74-year-old woman living in an assisted living home. Apparently, her husband of 45 years finally wanted out; seemed like an easy one.

The Play

I drove to the small town—it was up north, built into the hillsides. Seemed like a nice, fall day and a nice small town, until I got to my destination.

I arrived at the assisted living home and found it to be a secured apartment complex. With my badge hanging around my neck and papers in hand, I went inside to the lobby of the building. I looked at the directory and buzzer and saw that the only one labeled was the office button. I buzzed the office button and spoke with the manager. I told him who I was and what I was doing, and who I was looking for. He was cooperative and said he would send my old lady friend out to the front door.

As the frail old woman in a bathrobe came to the glass door, I told her I was a private detective. She looked at my badge as I told her, "Margaret—I have some papers here for you. Could you open the door for me?"

"No!" she yelled. "I don't want them! You can keep."

"Margaret, these are court documents and you have to take them," I told her, as she turned around and started to walk away. I've never seen an old woman move so fast.

I went back outside and happened to see a local police car driving through the parking lot. I flagged him down to talk, and explained to him my dilemma. He was friendly enough, so I asked him if he could help me get inside.

"I got an idea," he told me. "There's a retired police captain that lives in there. I'll give him a call and he can let you in." I went back inside the lobby, and after a few minutes, a really tall gray-haired gentleman came up to the door.

"Hi, I'm Frank. I'm a retired police captain from here in town, can I help you?" he asked.

"Do you know Margaret M.P?"

"Oh yes, I know Margaret," he said, looking at my badge.

"I'll let you in and take you to her apartment."

As we walked down the hallways, he eventually stopped in the middle of a long hallway and pointed to a door at the end of the hall. "That's her apartment. I'm going now as I don't want any trouble with any of the other residents."

I proceeded down and knocked on the door. It was quiet inside, so I called her name several times while knocking, "Margaret, this is the detective at the door—we have to talk."

Finally, I heard her inside—she must have been near the door and was apparently talking on the phone. I could hear her—it seemed she called a reverend.

"Reverend James, I need help!" she quipped. "My husband and I are not getting along. He doesn't love me anymore and there's a detective after me!"

"Margaret, I'm still here and I won't go away!" I slid the papers under the door, but they wouldn't go in all the way.

I think I was hitting her feet on the other side of the door. "I know you've got them now and you are officially served."

I walked quickly back to the lobby before the old bat had a chance to run after me. After getting dirty looks from some of the other residents, I finally made it back outside. Wow, fresh air again. Now I know why the old man was divorcing this crazy lady after 45 years. I started my long journey home, happy to complete this assignment. It wasn't as easy as I thought, but at least I got to meet one of the fastest ass-kicking old ladies on the planet.

Good Movie!
Who's Watching Who?

The Set Up

Another routine assignment up north. Serve some dead-beat dad behind on his child support (or lack thereof) with a court summons. I did a little research on him and it seemed he was shacking up with a girlfriend, north of the city, and was not paying his ex-wife her child support. As usual, though, I didn't get a photo or any description of him to identify him; just that he was 32 years old.

The Play

I headed up north, past the city, and ended up on a long, dusty road. I finally found the place and it wasn't pretty. It looked like a place Bonnie and Clyde held out back in the 30s. There were no cars and the house was dark. It was obvious no one was home. I headed back to the last small town I passed through to get a bite to eat.

After a while, I headed back to the love shack. As I passed the place for a look, I saw lights in the house go off and a car running in the driveway. I turned out down the road and got behind the car as it pulled out of the driveway.

I stayed back to give them some room. It looked like we were heading into town.

I was hoping they would stop at a gas station or some other quick stop where I could try to check the license plate and serve him. To my dismay, we ended up arriving at a movie theater. The car stopped at the front doors when I noticed that there were three people in the car. The male driver let out a male and female couple and then drove off to park the car. I got a good look at the couple, then drove over to where the driver had parked the car. He was already heading inside, so I parked a short distance away and went over to his rusty and dust covered Oldsmobile.

I looked inside for anything to identify the guy. *Shit.* Nothing but Burger King bags, a pile of cigs in the ashtray, and an empty bottle of *Jack Daniels* whiskey. I killed the flashlight and had to use my leather gloves to wipe the dust off the back plate to even read it. I wanted to run the plate with the boss, but after checking my cell phone and finding I have no reception here up north, I found out I was on my own and on my way to go see a movie.

The way things are going, I figured they were going to see a movie called *Life's a bitch, and then you die.* I walked inside and got in line, just behind the three suspects. I had to guess one of these two guys was my man. I stood behind them as they were looking up at the list of movies, trying to decide what to watch. The woman with them pointed out that she wanted to watch some stupid love story. I was in no mood for some goddamn chick flick, so I nudged up to the two guys and pointed up to *Die Hard.* "I heard that's a good one—the best Bruce Willis movie yet!"

All three turned around and looked at me. The woman gave me a dirty look while the two guys smiled, as though I was getting them out of having to watch some stupid movie. One thing I learned from their smiles: There must not be any dentists within a hundred miles.

I checked my phone again—still no reception. As I figured one of these two guys is my man, I decided to stay close and maybe hear them say each other's names. *What the hell*, I hadn't seen the new *Die Hard*, so I thought I'd just go in with them and catch a movie while getting paid for it. This way would be more fun—I could screw with him and serve him during the climax of the movie.

We went into the movie theater and I saw where they were sitting, so I went back out to the lobby area. Suddenly my phone rang. Luckily it was my boss wanting an update as to what was going on. I had him run the license plate, and a minute later, he told me the good news. This is our man. I figured now that the driver is likely the low life I was searching for.

I went back inside the theater to watch the movie. Hell, I already paid for the ticket and might as well finish a good movie. I sat a few rows behind the trio. The theater was almost full, and a good opportunity never arose for me to serve him while we were in there.

The movie finally ended and everyone started to head back to the lobby area. I was close behind my new friends, and as we got into the lobby area, I called out to my guy.

He swung his head around in surprise. "What?" he said back, wondering who I was.

"Wasn't that an exciting movie?" I asked him.

He seemed befuddled and said back, "Um, yea!"

"Well, if you thought that was exciting, I got something even more exciting for you! It's from the state of Wisconsin!"

I took the papers out of my back pocket and handed them to him. He took them and after a quick glance, his look of confusion turned into a look of anger.

"What the hell! I can't believe you sat and watched that whole movie with us and now you're serving me with papers?" he cried.

The woman also seemed perturbed and yelled at me, "I know we shouldn't have listened to you!" Then she yelled at her boyfriend, "I told you we should've gone to see *my* movie!"

As I walked away, I said to Billy, "You showed up on time for the movie, just make sure you show up on time for court—or the next movie you watch may be from jail."

They stood there looking at the papers as I walked out of the theater. I made it back to my car and quickly drove away. I drove down the dusty roads until I finally made it back to some kind of civilization and had a good signal on my phone. I called in the good news to my boss and headed south. I couldn't wait to get home and take a hot shower and wash away my thoughts of the toothless trio with a double shot of whiskey.

Guess Who's Coming to dinner

The Setup

This was supposed to be just another paper service. Serving a 20-year-old with a small claims summons. It was up north; one of those where the bastard better be home when I get there. So, one Thursday night I headed up north.

The Play

I arrived in the small town just after 5:00 in the afternoon on a cold fall day. The sun was hanging low in the sky. This was one of those towns where half of the house numbers were either faded out or just plain missing. So, I parked the car and set out on foot.

I approached the first house and was greeted by a large dog and his white not so pearly teeth. I asked the dog what the problem was—but he was no help. I showed no fear and walked up to the door, with my barking dog friend just behind me. I knocked on the door and was greeted by a friendly, small structured blonde in her forties. She was kind enough to put "killer," the dog, in the bathroom, then came back to the door and looked at the badge hanging around my neck.

"Can I help you, Detective?"

"Can I talk to Jason for a moment?"

"Jason is my son, and he's not here at the moment," she told me.

"When do you expect him back home?" I asked. "Why don't you come back around supper time and he should be back by then, in about an hour."

So, I went for a small walk to kill time and had a sandwich at one of those small-town mom and pop restaurants. I headed back, as it was now approaching 6:00 and I was hoping my friend Jason would be home by now. When I got back to the house, I got a rather pleasant surprise. Jason's mom answered the door again. "Oh hi, Detective. Jason's not home yet. I'm sorry, but would you like to come in for dinner?"

Um, I thought, trying to buy time to think about what to say.

I have to say, I've never been invited inside a house where I'm trying to serve papers.

What the hell, I was still hungry and she was kinda cute.

Before we could go inside, a car pulled up in the driveway. A large-framed older male got out of the car and walked up to us.

"Hi, Franklin!" she said to him. As it turned out, he was the town mayor and county Judge. We all go inside and sit down at the kitchen table. The mayor asked her if he could use the bathroom. I looked over at the bathroom and could still hear the dog barking inside it. It could have been my imagination, but I swear I saw the bathroom door handle turning back and forth as it seemed the dog was trying to get out.

Mom went over and opened the bathroom door and let the dog out, and the dog proceeded to relieve himself all over the kitchen floor. For some strange reason, the mayor changed his mind about the bathroom. He looked at his watch and proclaimed, "Ooops, I gotta go!" He walked out while Mom quickly cleaned up the mess on the floor. My appetite definitely faded away.

Mom walked over to the stove, where she had been cooking potatoes and meatloaf. "It's almost ready!"

"I have to go outside and make a phone call," I told her as I walked to the front door.

I walked outside, and lo and behold, Jason pulls up in his rusty old pickup truck.

He got out and we met in the driveway. *So,* I finally served Jason the court summons on behalf of the state of Wisconsin. I walked up to the front door with Jason and as he entered, I yelled to his mother, "Thank you for the offer for dinner but I have to go now!"

I left; *as the dinner was starting to smell like potatoes and dog piss anyway,* I thought as I pulled out of the driveway and started the long way back home.

Hat Trick

It was a cloudy, dreary day when Gabe and I got our assignments for the day.

"I have a surveillance case to work today," Gabe told me as we walked from the office and looked up at snow coming down upon us.

"Have fun with that. I hope the heater is working in the van. I have 3 papers to serve up in Wright County."

We bid each other good luck and went our ways.

Number 1

I drove to my first assignment. I had to serve a Kelly R. with a subpoena to appear as a witness in a dog biting incident.

I arrived at the duplex as the sun was going down.

I grabbed the paperwork from my leather briefcase and walked up to the front door. I pushed the doorbell button, but didn't hear anything. I waited a moment to see if anyone would appear, but as no one responded, I knocked on the door.

Another moment passed with no answer. As I knocked harder, the door flung open while I was still knocking, and my fist nearly hit the large man that had opened the door.

Now, I am a large man myself, but this guy was a giant. I was amazed at his size as I looked up at him.

"Um, hi," I stammered. He caught me off-guard and I stuttered in his presence as I told him I was looking for Kelly.

He didn't speak and just stared down at me.

"Is she at home?" I asked him.

He remained silent, looking at me like a small wooden peg he was about to pound into the ground.

"I just need to talk to her for a second," I continued.

He leaned forward, now only a few inches from my face, and finally spoke, "You dumb bastard. I'm Kelly."

My hands were shaking as I handed him the subpoena. "Sorry," I told him. "*So*, could you give these to her?" I told him, so rattled that I was in a daze. "Mean, these are for you."

He finally swiped them out of my hand and I quickly backed away, almost tripping on the sidewalk. It took a while to get my composure back. I got back into my car, not looking back and trying to forget the whole ordeal. I gathered enough courage to head off to my next assignment.

Number 2

I had the map all laid out. I got into the next town and found the address easily. It was a new development—new homes where two years ago, corn grew for miles. I stopped a few blocks away to read through and organize the papers. My destination was the residence of a Jeff and Rita M.

I had to serve Jeff with a subpoena and paternity suit— apparently his potent sperm was well placed in someone besides Rita. As a result, the other woman was forcing him to court to take a paternity test. I figured that once I served Jeff, there was going to be no way I was shaking his hand I know where it's been.

I pulled up to the house and parked in the street. It was dark now and the house was well lit. The garage door was open, and as I walked up the driveway, I could see a car inside with the hood up. I got closer to see a man and woman under the hood working on the car. There was a wooden, carved-out plaque on the wall which read, *The M.'s—Jeff and Rita*, with detailed little hearts and flowers surrounding their names. I seemed to startle them when I walked into the garage and shouted, "Hello!"

They both jumped up. "Are you Jeff?" I asked the male.

"Yes," he said, staring at the shiny badge around my neck.

His female companion glared into my eyes and said, "What's this all about?"

"Well, Jeff," I said to him. "Can I talk to you alone for a few minutes?"

"Sure, I guess," he said back.

"No, no—I'm his wife and I want to know what this is for."

I waited for Jeff to say something—but as they both just looked at me like a *Bambi* on the highway, I continued, "Well, Jeff—I have a subpoena here for you, and an attached paternity lawsuit," I told him as I handed the papers to him.

Rita's eyebrows went up while her jaw dropped down. "What the fuck is going on?" she said, now raising her voice and grabbing the papers away from him. Jeff didn't need to read them. I could tell he knew what and whom it was all about.

I wanted to exit in a quick way, so I finished by telling Jeff, "There is a court date set as it states in the subpoena that you need to go to."

I started backing out of the garage as I could feel Rita's blood beginning to boil.

"What the fuck did you do now?" she screamed at him. "You knocked up some bitch? My God, you fucking pig! Who in the hell is Sheila?"

As I walked back to my car, I took a look back as I could hear Rita still giving it to Jeff—who just stood there silently taking it all in—as if he finally knew he was caught and his little secret is over. I glanced one last time at the wooden plaque on the wall, and shook my head as I drove away.

Suspicious Person

My cell phone rang. I looked at the caller ID and saw that it was Mark. Again. Trouble in paradise. Again. I only answered because the son of a bitch owed me a lot of money from the last time I did surveillance on that crazy, untamed bitch wife of his.

"Hello, Mark," I answered.

Before I could say anything else, he started ranting, "I need you to watch Misty tonight. I just know she's gonna have that fuckin' boyfriend over again tonight and she's not supposed to have him there when our kids are there!"

I could hear his heart beating through the phone. I reminded him of the money he still owed, "Mark, we've been doing surveillance on her for two years. She knows we watch her. She looks for us every day whether we are watching her or not. Even at Christmas time." He didn't care. I didn't either, as long as this prick paid me in the end.

So, after another promise of being paid next Friday, I ignored my doubts and decided to do it. Besides, I think it was going to be another full moon tonight.

I headed out in the late afternoon. The house was not an easy place to do surveillance. New house, new development, cul-de-sac and turnabouts, no trees, and lots of pretentious rich assholes lurking about. It's hard to hide my surveillance van amongst the Jaguars and Mercedes Benzes parked in the area. I managed to wedge myself between two houses empty and under construction.

I violated the first rule of surveillance: Never park where the subject can see you from their house. This time, however, I had no choice but this is the best I could do.

She was home—good thing she had too much shit in the garage to park inside, so her luxury car being in the driveway, I knew she was home.

A few hours later, a convertible pulled up to the house. Misty came out of the house and jumped in the passenger seat. I watched them drive away through my binoculars. I was now in the front seat as I was preparing to follow them.

I waited a moment as they appeared to be heading my way. Before I knew it, they stopped right next to my van. Misty jumped out and started pointing her finger at me and screamed at me, "Who the hell do you think you are?" In the same breath, she yelled, "I already called the police on you."

Sure enough, a squad car was approaching. Just to fuck with her, I got out of the van holding the binoculars. "What are you talking about?" I said to her.

She looked at my binoculars in disbelief. "Have you been watching me before?"

I chuckled as the officer approached and she backed off. The officer told her to get back in her car as he would handle this now. The girls drove away in their fancy car and I talked to the city's finest.

"What are you doing out here?" he asked me. I tossed the binoculars back inside the van—figuring I had enough fun with them taunting Misty. I showed the officer my badge and ID, and told him I was out here on public property on a legal assignment. Another rule of surveillance: Never tell a cop who you are watching. Especially in smaller towns.

Leaving the names out, I told him my story. He smiled, and after some small talk, he left. I guess I was done for tonight. I knew what was going to happen next. Misty went home, called Mark and bragged about catching me out there. Sure enough, before I could even start the van, Mark called me up all excited and ranting about how Misty was saying something about catching a rat and laughing at him.

"What happened out there?" he panicked.

"What the hell do you think happened?" I snapped back at him. "I warned you that she looks for someone watching her. I told you that it is impossible to watch her, especially at this goddamn new house she's in, and—" he cut me off, saying he had to go because Misty was calling him again.

I told him I would talk to him tomorrow. I couldn't handle talking to him anymore tonight anyway. I headed back to the office, ready for a good stiff drink. Or two. Or five.

So, the next Friday, the local newspaper comes out and I'm reading it in the office. I looked across the local police reports for the week. I happened to see a report about a suspicious person call. It would seem that a local 38-year-old woman called the police about a man she thought was…

Jeffrey J (Frank L.)

Part 1

The summer was dragging on. The heat and humidity was getting to all of us. We were looking for a break from the heat by filling a cooler with beer and going out fishing for some bass and a buzz.

After we had our fill, we docked the boat. An old friend of ours was also on the dock, just getting ready to go out. Dave was an insurance lawyer who had given us work in the past. I hadn't heard from him in a while, so we did a little catching up before Dave starting talking about work. "Hey guys," he said. "I have a case for you. How would you like it if I pay for the two of you to go on a fishing trip?"

We looked at each other and smiled. "We'd be glad to go fishing for you—it will be a good business trip. It sounds interesting."

We were eager to pack our suitcases, fishing equipment, and cameras—then loaded our guns with ammo. We were all set for the next day.

Part 2

We got a few hours of sleep, then headed out in the middle of the night for the Badlands of the Dakotas. The trip was longer than we had planned. We were already tired as we drove into town. I immediately drove to the address we had for Frank L. Gabe, stayed in town, and went to the only place that was open—the local café. He was going to get some breakfast and information about our Mr. Frank L.

He lived on the edge of town—neither one of us had any bars on our cell phones, so we had to use our backup CB radios to communicate. I drove past Frank L.'s house—it was a small rambler with a closed garage. There weren't any vehicles outside and no lights on inside. I parked down the road, and made small talk with Gabe on the radio to pass the time.

Around noon, a young male exited the rear entrance of the house and walked out to get the mail. He went back inside, and I took the opportunity to go and knock on the back door. The kid answered—and told me he was just renting out the basement from Frank L. He said he hadn't seen him in weeks, and that he was probably gone fishing somewhere. I met up with Gabe, who found out that Frank L. liked fishing and was friends with the local chief of police.

So, it was off to the local Police Station. We had to wait outside until 9 am, when someone finally came to open up the place. We went inside to talk to the Chief. He was a very large man, sitting behind his desk and puffing on a big cigar. Friendly guy. Typical small-town USA. Turned out, he was really good friends with Frank L. Even more, he told us that

Frank was a fishing guide on the Missouri River and even gave us directions to the trailer home where he stayed at.

We easily found the trailer park near the river. Gabe had already traced his vehicle information, and found out which trailer number Frank was living and working out of. I drove past his comfy little trailer, but there was no sign of Frank or his pickup truck.

Gabe, who remained back in town to keep an eye on his residence—in case he doubled back on us. He had looked up local maps and told me that there was a boat landing just a few miles from town. By "town," I mean 20 trailers and a bar.

I drove out to the boat landing on the river, and son of a bitch, I couldn't believe my eyes. After searching for Frank for two days, I finally found his rusty old truck, with an empty boat trailer attached.

I was in the middle of nowhere; yet there was a pay telephone at the boat landing. It was hard to believe. I scanned the river and didn't see any boats coming in. I was so excited that I had to call Gabe and our client to give them the good news. The bad news was that there was no cell phone signal, and the CB radios wouldn't work because we were too far apart.

I was panicking to find enough change—I had to at least talk to Dave, the lawyer, and our client. I needed to get authorization from him to go ahead with surveillance for at least another day. I reached into my pocket for quarters. To my amazement, I had three quarters I could use for the payphone. I hoped it was enough.

As I was talking to Dave, he couldn't believe that I had tracked Frank down, that I was in the middle of nowhere, and I was talking on a pay telephone next to the Missouri River in the Dakotas.

"You have an open checkbook. Just make sure you have your camera ready when Frank comes back."

"I'll be ready," I assured him.

I found a parking spot at the top of the hill with a good view of the river and boat landing. There was little cover, but it would be worth it.

Part 3

A few hours went by, when I spotted something on the river heading my way. Suddenly, he was upon me. There he was, in all his glory. Bad back and all. The scammer that he is—if he only knew that I was filming him from our undercover van, and recording his every move.

My face lit up with a big smile as he lifted the heavy fishing gear out of the boat with his "bad back." The best was yet to come, as his male companion stood on the boat ramp and letting Frank bust his phony ass.

Eventually, Frank managed to load his fishing boat onto the trailer, it was such a sight for my sore eyes, (and Frank's 'sore' back), that I was constantly checking the camera to make sure it was recording. Frank finally finished tying down his boat when he and his fishing buddy stood outside talking. At one point, they pointed up towards me, then got in the truck and drove up off the boat ramp. My heart started beating harder when I realized they were not heading back into town, but up the hill towards me. I jumped in the front seat and pretended to be talking on my cell phone when Frank pulled up next to me.

"Do you need any help?" he asked me.

"No, thanks, but I'm just trying to reach my Dad. He's gonna try and make it up here this weekend and take me out fishing," I told him.

"Well, I tell you what. I'm actually a fishing guide here on the river, and I can take you out too, in case he doesn't make it," Frank explained. "I might just take you up on that."

"Well, there's a nice, small motel in town you can stay at, and we go to the bar every night. Maybe I'll see you there later on," Frank said.

"OK, I'll see you there," I told him.

He then drove off and headed back into town.

Part 4
The Bar

With such a view of the river and "town," I stayed out there for a few more hours. Frank was staying put in his trailer, so I drifted into town and got a room at the small, creepy motel. It reminded me of an old Alfred Hitchcock movie. The sweet old lady at the front desk greeted me with a big smile, revealing a big black wad of chewing tobacco. She showed me my room, and I was glad to find it had electricity.

"I'm Darla," she said to me, standing outside the open front door. "If you need anything, sweetie," she continued, while spitting on the ground, "You just give me a call."

She apparently didn't realize that there was a wad of tobacco that went with that spitball, and splattered all over her shoes as she gave me a wink and walked away.

I spent a few hours charging my batteries and preparing my hidden camera and microphone in my front shirt pocket. It was dark out now, so I decided to walk over to the bar. It was a larger bar, with pool tables and dart boards on one side and tables for eating on the other.

The bar itself was in the middle—a half-circle made out of beautiful hand carved oak. Of course, this was ruined by the cheap and ripped up barstools around it.

I found Frank sitting at the bar. As I approached him, he greeted me with a big, "Hey! You made it!"

I sat down next to him and ordered a tap beer. We made small talk at first, with Frank asking about my dad and where I'm from. I couldn't wait too long before switching the conversation over to his fishing activities.

With my hidden camera and microphone literally 2 feet away from his mouth, Frank went on to tell me how he's been a fishing guide on the river for 15 years. He explained that he used to drive a semi-truck for a major shipping company, but wanted to start a fishing guide business here. "So," Frank went on to say, "I pretended to have a back injury so I could keep on getting a check while I'm out here."

I leaned into Frank with my hidden gear while he talked, making sure he was speaking right into the microphone. The female bartender soon came over to refill our beer mugs.

"Lisa here," Frank said while pointing at the smiling bartender, "Also has a bad back." They both laughed about it.

"Yeah," Lisa said. "I gotta go see one of them insurance company doctors in about a month, and I'm not looking forward to that."

"Well, I have an appointment next week, and I can't wait to tell them damn insurance company doctors to kiss my brown, hairy ass! I feel pretty good now, but I know how to act in front of those doctors. I know how to keep the insurance checks coming in."

"Frank!" someone yelled from across the bar. "You're up!" Frank got up off the barstool and walked over to the dartboards, and spent about an hour playing. It was fun to watch as he easily moved about, constantly bending over to pick darts up off the floor. After the game, he came back and sat down next to me at the bar.

Once again, I steered the conversation towards his fishing, his boat, and he invited me to go out on the river the next day with him.

"Well, I'm gonna wait and see if my dad shows up," I told him. "I might just wait up on that hill again—it's the only place I can get a cell phone signal. So, if I don't hear from him, you go on ahead without me."

We continued talking for a while, then Frank said goodnight and left the bar. I soon left as well, and walked back to my hotel room, making sure to side step the still wet tobacco on the ground.

The following morning, I got up early and drove out to my surveillance position on the hill. From a distance, I could see Frank's bright, red truck next to his trailer. Hours went by and I was losing hope. Finally, however, I noticed his truck leaving his trailer, with the boat attached. He stopped for a short while at the bar, then headed out to the boat landing. He was by himself, and I enjoyed watching, and recording Frank as he backed his trailer into the water and was lifting his heavy boat and maneuvering it off the trailer. It was a windy day, so Frank was having a hell of a time trying to do it by himself. He eventually headed out and down the river a short distance. He spent about twenty minutes fishing where I could still see him, then slowly drifted down river and out of view.

A few hours later he returned—and again spent some time fishing near the boat ramp, then again loaded his boat on the trailer. It was great film work and I couldn't wait for my partner, Gabe, to see this video, as well as the judge and the insurance company that was issuing his work comp checks.

Oh yeah, we also couldn't wait for Frank to see the video in court—I guess we'll be buying the popcorn.

Is There A Doctor In The House?

Is There a Doctor in The Blouse?

1. The Set up

Sitting at the desk in the office, scouring the internet for deadbeats, I heard a light knock on the open door. She walked in, wiping tears from her eyes. She was an older lady, about 50 and a little frumpy. She sat at the chair in front of my desk and I offered her a tissue. I asked her what was going on.

"It's my husband," she gives a big sigh and continues. "He's a doctor. He...he told me that there was a doctors' convention this weekend down in the city and that he needs to attend. Something about new procedures or something."

I just kept quiet as she wiped her tears, then continued, "I called down there and...and...and found out it's really a nurses' convention."

I continued to remain silent.

"You see, he's got an old girlfriend. She's a nurse. They know each other from high school and...and..."

"That's OK, take your time," I told her.

"I've suspected he was cheating on me with her a few years ago. And now he's acting the same weird way and being secretive. I want you to follow him down there and keep an eye on him this weekend."

So, after getting a retainer and more info about her husband, the old girlfriend, and signing a few forms, we made our plan.

"It's our daughter's birthday on Friday," she said. "We are having a party for her in the afternoon when he gets home. He plans on leaving then around 6:00, so you would have to follow him from our house down to the city. I don't know where he's staying. He told me he would call me when he finds a hotel and gets settled in."

So, that was the plan. After checking their address on the map and seeing they live out in the country, I knew this wasn't going to be easy following someone from there all the way down to the city. I also got as much information about the convention as possible. It starts Saturday morning.

Friday comes—slept in late and woke up with a massive hangover. Time to prep for the weekend. Fill the van up with gas. Make sure the camera and camcorder batteries are charged. Snacks, piss bottle, some cash, maps, extra clothes. Gotta get a good look at the state map—guessing which way we are gonna take from his house to the city. Also, gotta study where hotels are in the city in case I lose him on the way. Not much info was available on the net about this convention—it's downtown and there are 4 hotels nearby.

Ihead out and arrive at the home just before 5:00. *Shit.* Way out in the boonies and a long driveway leading into the woods—can't see their house. Luckily, there was an intersection about a half mile away. That meant I could sit at the stop sign, use the binoculars and watch the end of his driveway for him to leave.

Right on cue, just a few minutes after six, a brown Lincoln Continental departed—just what my client said he'd be driving. He pulls onto the main road and drives away from me. I gotta hit it to get behind him. And so, the cat and mouse game is on; though the mouse doesn't know the cat is sneaking around behind him. It's a delicate game following someone in car—deciding how far to stay back, how to play the stoplights, stop signs, other cars getting between us. You can't screw this up—if he catches on that he's being followed then the case is over. You're done. He won't do what he planned now, he may assume his wife put us on his tail and lash out at her.

Or, if we lose him, it's a mad scramble to try and find him. If you don't find him, you don't get paid, client is pissed, and you go home for the weekend with your head down low and empty handed.

Luckily, this one was going well. I stayed back, followed for a while until we got onto the freeway leading right to the city. Lots of traffic on this Friday evening. He's driving pretty fast, which meant I often had to cut people off, weave in and out of traffic to keep the right distance and his car in view, drive fast then drive slow—surely pissing off dozens of other drivers thinking I'm an idiot driver. I've seen more middle fingers that a manicurist.

Finally, after about an hour, we finally make it to the city. He pulls into a Holiday Inn and parks near the front door. I hang back, but gotta be quick as I want to see what room he is assigned. No spots close except handicapped ones, so I gotta park in one of them and walk quickly inside.

I enter the lobby and see that he is waiting at the front desk, with one person in front of him. That was definitely him—matching the picture of him his wife gave me. A little chubby and not very attractive. I sat at one of the chairs in the lobby, baseball hat on and hooded sweatshirt. After a few minutes, the doctor stepped up to the desk and starting checking in. I had to time this perfectly to find out what room he would be assigned. After a minute, I walked up to the desk and stood next to him.

"I'll help you in a minute sir," she told me.

"No, hurry." I took out my checkbook and pretended to keep busy. I noted, as he spoke to the clerk, that his voice was very distinct—deep and with a slight lisp. After a few more minutes, I could see the clerk writing down his room number on the small card key envelope. As she slid it across the desk, I made my move. I turned their way and managed to discretely peek over and see the room number as I then walked back to the chair. Room 512. And, I noticed he had only one card key.

"I can help you now, sir."

"OK. I'm gonna wait a few minutes here for my wife," I told her.

I wanted to give my doctor friend a few minutes to get settled in. After about five minutes, I went up to the desk.

So, we started the process. As I wanted to get a room next to my friend, I asked the clerk, "You know, me and my wife were here 2 years ago for our anniversary. Is there a way I can surprise her and get the same room?"

"If the room is available, sir, I can certainly help you with that. What room number was it?" she asked.

"I think it was 511. Or maybe it was 501. I'm sorry, I should remember that. No, it was 511."

She looks on the computer. "I'm sorry, sir. We are pretty booked due to a convention next door. I have only two rooms available: 302 or 101. Both have one queen size bed."

Shit. Now what am I gonna do. Neither one helps. May as well take the one on the first floor. So, I check in. I go back out to the van—luckily still in the handicap spot. After a few dirty looks from others nearby, I move the van, grab my bags and quickly go to my room. I grab just what I need: Extra batteries, extra 8mm blank videotapes, some cash and the "hidden camera." In those days, we didn't have camera phones, teeny cameras or anything fancy. Maybe the big city PIs or guys in the CIA had better stuff, but all I had was an 8mm camcorder with a pinhole lens and a tailored fanny pack with a small pinhole. I also rigged a small wired microphone plugged into the camera and poking out a hole in the side of the fanny pack. Yes, I would be the dork walking around with a large fanny pack around my waist. I have to wear it loose so that I can swing it around and point it in the direction of the activity I need to record. I change clothes, take off the cap and try to change my appearance in any possible way—I never saw my friend take a good look at me in the lobby but you never know. Now I'm ready to go. I head up to the fifth floor.

2. The Play

It was very quiet on the fifth floor. I walked past 512 and could hear the TV on. I paused and could hear the water faucet turn on for a few seconds. Two good things: He was still here and you could hear what's going on inside. I also noticed that there was a large gap at the bottom of the door and the floor. I listened for a while to make sure he was alone. As I heard no talking for a while—I assumed he was alone.

I took the elevator down to the lobby to assess the area. I step off the elevator and look around. To the right was the front desk and the main entrance. To the left was another exit—which I later found out led to the convention center and a strip club next door. Straight ahead was the hotels bar. This was good—I could sit at the bar and watch the elevator. I would at least be able to see him leaving and follow him.

I sat at the bar and ordered a stiff drink. I thought about all the different scenarios. This nurse could already have a room here. I don't know what she looks like, so she could walk right past me without me knowing it. She could be the woman sitting across the bar from me. I could be there all weekend with my eyes poking out and nothing would ever happen. I could only choose the path that covers as many scenarios. I chose to sit at the bar and watch the elevator, while going up to check on my friend every so often to see if I could hear anything.

Six drinks later, about an hour and a half, the elevator doors open and my doctor friend begins to step out. I turn away, using peripheral vision to see that he is walking straight into the bar. I keep my side to him as he walks in— and looks around, obviously looking for someone. After a moment, he turns around and walks toward the back exit. Keeping distance, I follow him—hanging back as I see him walk out the hotel and to the strip joint next door. I go back to the hotel bar, finish my drink and slowly walk to the strip joint.

I walked inside the titty bar and immediately saw my friend sitting ringside. I was never one for the first-row seating, so it was no problem for me to grab a seat at the bar in the back to keep an eye on my doctor friend. Yeah, sure my eyes were mostly kept on the beautiful women dancing and walking around naked—I didn't think my friend was gonna hook up with his nurse friend at a strip club. I had a feeling, that by this time, she was either gonna show up late tonight or tomorrow morning. Maybe this guy just wanted a weekend away from his wife?

After about an hour, he got up and left. I trailed behind as he walked back to the hotel and got on the elevator. I went back to the bar for a quick drink, and after about five minutes, I took the elevator up to the fifth floor. I walked past his room and could hear the TV on inside, but nothing else. So, I had to play the waiting game. I took out my room card key and my cell phone and held them in my hand—then waited a few doors down. As the rest of the floor was quiet—I just stood near one of the doors. When someone would come up off the elevator, I would pretend to be fumbling for my keys and talking on my cell, stalling until they entered their room. Occasionally, I'd walk past the doctor's room to listen. Eventually the TV went off and all was quiet. I continued this until 3 am, and decided nothing was going to happen tonight at his point. I returned to my room and got a few hours of sleep.

The convention was to start at 8 am—so I got up at 7 and gave a quick walk past the doctor's room. All quiet. I went down to the lobby—saw the bar was closed—and decided to sit in a lobby chair. I picked up a newspaper and played the old trick of hiding behind the paper, reading it while peeking out at anyone getting off the elevator.

Finally, around 8:30, my friend got off the elevator and headed out. He walked to the convention center, and I gave him plenty of room as I was not going inside. If he was gonna screw someone, it wasn't going to happen in there. I sat on a bench with my newspaper, with a good view of the entrance to the convention center, and waited. And waited.

It wasn't until 4:30 in the afternoon when he finally walked back out, alone, and to the hotel. He took the elevator up, and I gave him some time. About 20 minutes later, I took the elevator up—as there was only one elevator, I wasn't worried about missing him leaving. I just was hoping not to meet him on the damn thing. A walk past his room this time, there was a different sound, it was not the sound of a TV, it was the sound of someone talking on a phone. Just then, a woman two doors down, came out into the hallway. I greeted her with a smile and walked to the elevator and got in. Thinking to myself, could that be the doctor's lover? Maybe he was talking on the phone in his room to her. I got off the elevator and headed for my favorite spot in the bar overlooking the elevator door. After two or three crown royal whiskeys, I got a big surprise. Who should step out of the elevator but the woman I greeted upstairs with a smile and the doctor! Then I headed for the back door of the bar. Now that they were still in the bar together downing some alcoholic beverages, I took that time to go to the trunk of my car to get a special briefcase. This custom briefcase has a round hole in the very bottom end of the briefcase. An 8mm camcorder fits in there real nice. Then I walked back into the Holiday Inn with my briefcase in hand. Back inside, I decided to grab a newspaper for the day. Then I proceeded to find a chair in the main lobby facing the main inside entrance to the bar. After patiently sitting in that damn chair for over an hour, it paid off. Who walks out of the bar with their arms around each other? None other than the doctor and his lady lover, the nurse. Now at this point in time, I had the 8 mm camcorder running and filing that lovely couple. Now they headed for the outside door to the parking lot. The briefcase and I followed them to the parking lot; once outside, I got lucky, for there was a park bench overlooking the parking lot, where the doctor had his car parked. I picked up my newspaper and pretended to read it as I had my 8 mm running in my briefcase facing the doctor's car. I saw the women push her body into the doctor's body they stood there by the doctor's car, making out hot and heavy with kissing and passionately pressing their bodies very close to each other. I'm thinking I got what I need for my work, I left the lovers to go at it in the parking lot and went back into the Holiday Inn and processed to check myself out of the hotel and pay my bill. Walking out of the Holiday Inn towards my car with luggage in hand, I couldn't help but think how bold the lovers were in broad daylight. But this way, I got my evidence. It was a long drive back to the detective office in River Falls in the pouring rain. When I got to the River Falls office and used the phone, I said, "Hey, this is Gabe, big Steve, I got the job done, watching the doctor and with plenty of evidence. Our lady client will be happy we caught the doctor in the act of cheating.

Big Steve said, "Gabe, we got to go out and celebrate this assignment."

The happy ending was that the doctor's wife paid us well for this assignment.

Cedar Avenue Coin Collector

Part 1

The Set up

I was at the desk, ready to open the bottom drawer for my top shelf Brandy, trying to forget about the assignment I had the night before. Then the phone rang. I could see on the caller ID that it was my biggest client—one of the biggest law firms in the state. I had a bad feeling about this because they never give me any easy cases.

They wanted me to serve some high roller coin collector named Vincent in the city. I was right. This wasn't going to be easy because we might have to do surveillance and chase him down because apparently, he was tipped off and knew that someone was coming for him with a subpoena to testify in a trial that he didn't want anything to do with. That someone, unfortunately, was me.

I started up the Lincoln and headed into the city. This was going to be a two-man assignment, so I had to pick up one my partners on the way. Big Louie is always good to have around for a case like this, although we would probably have to stop at every fast-food joint on the way there.

The Journey

It was cold and rainy that morning. We parked the Lincoln down the road and walked up to the coin store. It was located in a luxurious building with other lavish stores inside. As we approached the store, I could immediately tell we were not dressed for the occasion.

I spotted Vincent's Mercedes Benz parked out front, so I stayed in the hallway and sent Big Louie in first so I could keep an eye on the car. From where I was standing, I could see through the tinted glass that Vincent wasn't in the store front, so he must have been in the back. I could see Louie pacing around and asking the female saleswomen questions. From a distance, I could tell they were intimidated by his appearance. As the minutes ticked away, I was getting worried because it didn't look like it was going very well.

Louie finally walked out of the store and still had the subpoena tucked away in his leather jacket. We met down the hall, out of view from the store front.

"What happened?" I asked Louie.

"Those damn bitches were lying and saying Vincent wasn't there. I know he's probably hiding in the back, watching the security cameras."

"OK," I told him, "I'll bet he isn't going to come out front, so let's keep an eye on his car,"

A few minutes went by when all hell broke loose. The main doors of the building blasted open and I could see seven policemen coming towards us with guns drawn. "Raise your hands, Louie—stay calm and don't move."

I knew there would be extra trouble because I had a loaded gun on me. With my arms in the air and the police approaching, I yelled out, " I have a gun on me and a permit for it."

One officer slammed me up against the wall and held me tight while another officer reached in and took my gun out of my shoulder holster. He asked me where my identification was, and I told him it was in my back pocket. He took my wallet and found my gun permit card and driver's license. The cop holding me noticed the chain around my neck and pulled out my badge and ID that I had around my neck, under my shirt. At this time, they realized I was one of the good guys.

I turned my head and saw Big Louie laying spread eagle on the floor with five policemen holding him down. I yelled out, "That's my partner!"

While they were searching the big guy, I explained to the cop near me why we were there and that the subpoena was inside Louie's jacket. I explained to them that we were trying to serve Vincent, the owner, inside the coin shop. The police apologized and told me that the two sales ladies inside the store said that two men were there and were attempting to rob the place.

"I bet they called you guys to buy time for Vincent," I told them.

They finally let Louie up off the floor. The sergeant took the subpoena from him and said, "Let's go back inside the store together."

We walked up to the saleswomen and the sergeant told them, "These guys are OK—they're detectives and are here to serve a subpoena on Vincent, your boss. Where is he?"

They told us that Vincent wasn't in and was gone for the day. The Sergeant said, "OK," and we walked out of the store.

We met up with Louie and the other officers in the hallway. I glanced out into the street and saw that the Mercedes was gone. Damn it. The little bastard got away. We all had a little chuckle about the whole event and went our own ways. We left town, and after a McDonalds run for Big Louie, I dropped him off at his house. I headed back to the office, as I couldn't wait to get to that bottom drawer.

Part 2

A month later, while sitting at the desk in the office, Big Louie walked in and plopped a newspaper in front of me.

"What's this about?" I asked him.

"Remember Vincent, the coin dealer? Check this headline out."

I picked up the paper and couldn't believe my eyes. The headline read, *Minnesota Coin Dealer Loses $4 Million in Hotel Heist Knife-wielding robbers escape after waylaying brother-in-law at annual show in Orlando, Florida.*

The article went on:

In the rare coin trade, the bad guys are fast, organized, and sometimes violent. Dealers drive with an eye on the rear-view mirror and change travel routes so they won't be easy marks. Even those safeguards, though, couldn't keep a Minnesota dealer from being robbed Saturday of some $4 million in coins. Thieves held his brother-in-law at knifepoint as they pulled bags of coins and records out of his friend's SUV in front of a busy luxury hotel in Orlando, Florida—a place dealers considered a "safe zone."

The suspects remain at large and, though they're likely in Florida, the dealer fears for his and his family's safety. He declined an interview and asked that his name not be used.

"Once you've been robbed, there's nobody who can tell you they're not coming back," said Laura Sperber, a fellow coin dealer, friend, and occasional business partner of the Minnesota Collector.

"They're deeply in shock," she said of the family. "It's the first time he's been robbed," she added. "It's a very traumatic thing when you get violated like that."

The attack by three masked robbers came in the lobby driveway of the Peabody Hotel about 6 pm. Hundreds of dealers were in Orlando for the Florida United Numismatists annual show, one of the largest in the country.

"It would be the equivalent of going to a Vikings game and robbing a Vikings player during the game," said Sperber. "It was that brazen a robbery."

The dealer walked into the hotel lobby while his brother-in-law, who works for the dealer, unloaded cases from the back of an SUV. He was grabbed from behind by a robber wearing a surgical mask and hooded sweater and forced to the ground with a knife to his throat, according to an Orange County Sheriff's report. An assailant also threatened a bellman who came to the man's aid. The robbers sped off, followed by a black truck, and couldn't be *spotted, according to the report. The license plate on the getaway car was registered to a person in Miami and fingerprints were lifted off the SUV, but authorities hadn't reached any conclusions Wednesday.*

"We're still following up on some things, looking at the video to see if they can pinpoint as to actually what happened," Deputy Carlos Padilla said. The coins were insured, but it was not clear for how much.

Organizers had stepped up security at the convention center where the show was held because of thefts last year. Even so, one other Minnesotan who had gone to the show and also asked not to be identified said he was nervous. The show's promoters, he said, had sent out letters in advance telling us things, like, "Be cautious and if your car gets bumped on the freeway, don't stop. Watch for cars trying to box you in, things like that."

The conventions, said Sperber, are a necessary part of the coin business; even in the internet age, people still need to see the goods. Dealers also are worried because the thieves took off with business records and a Rolodex of names. Sperber thinks this attack will bring a new safety focus.

If there's any consolation, she added, it's that the coins that were stolen are extremely rare and highly identifiable. As for the victim, Sperber said, his friends will help him reestablish his business. "Mentally, he needs time to heal."

I looked up at Louie and saw he had a huge grin on his face. "I think the insurance company needs time to heal, after paying this scamming son of a bitch four million dollars," I told Louie.

"Looks like an organized inside Italian job to me," Louie said. "I bet Vincent and his buddies are getting a big chuckle over this one. It's faster than trying to sell four million dollars' worth of coins. You get a big fat check from the insurance company, and because of the fake heist, they get their coins back too!"

"We'll have to keep this file open," I told Louie. "I'll put it right down here in the bottom drawer, next to the Brandy bottle."

It looks like crime pays after all?

Man Shoots at Gabe

The Set up

New assignment today. Warrant papers to serve on a Jason, a younger guy up north. North of Highway 8. I hate going north of the highway, as you seem to go back in time a hundred years. Nothing but wood ticks, meth labs, and lots of idiots with guns. The client thought Jason was living in Florida, but might be currently staying at his Mom's house up in northern Wisconsin. I checked Jason's driving record, and found that 10 days ago he got a speeding ticket 2 miles from the county line near his mom's house. So, I assumed he was up there. *Damn.* Florida is much nicer this time of year. So, north I go.

The Play

I headed up north. Once north of the highway, the cell phone signal was as scarce as teeth on a local. I proceeded on one dirt road after another. There were few fire numbers on the long driveways, and few numbers on the mailboxes.

I narrowed it down to one—possibly my boy's driveway. The numbers on the mailbox were so faded I had to make sure. Hey, what do you know—the mailbox was open and there were letters inside. What are the odds of that? I peeked at the name on one of the letters and confirmed this was the place.

I got back in my car, and just as I got settled in, I saw a light blue Ford pickup drive past me and go up the driveway. I followed the cloud of dust up the driveway, giving the driver a little space. After going over several hills on this long driveway, I finally made it to a clearing. There was an old farmhouse on the right, with a few older sheds all surrounded by pine trees.

I noticed the Ford truck stopped and parked by the house. A woman with a stocking hat opened the truck door and quickly ran inside the house, not bothering to close the truck door. I had a bad feeling about this and stopped short of the yard. Before I could do anything, a stocky man in a flannel shirt and dark sunglasses came out the front door, with a high-powered deer rifle mounted on his shoulder, aiming it at me. I'm not getting paid enough for this shit.

I decided not to stay, so I ducked down and quickly turned my car around and it was time to make my own dust clouds. As I headed back down the driveway, I could see the house in my rear-view mirror disappearing. I could also hear the gunshots whistling through the pine trees as I drove on. I clutched my own .45 auto at my side, but I wasn't in the mood for a shootout. I was finally out of his shooting range and made it to the "main road." With no cell phone signal, I headed into the nearest town.

I wasn't sure if anyone was following me, so I found a self-serve car wash and parked inside one of the empty stalls. It looked like the coast was clear. I finally had a signal on my cell phone—so I called *911* to try and reach the sheriff. I got through to dispatch, and spoke with a female deputy. I told her my story, but she thought it was a prank call. I had to convince her that I was a real private detective and would like some backup, as I wanted to go back to get my job done. I had to give her my badge number, license number and everything but my blood pressure levels, which were rising by the second.

Finally, three squad cars arrived at the car wash. The officer's jumped out with full battle gear on. I told them my story, and they agreed to follow me out there, after I showed him the papers I was trying to serve. The sergeant and I exchanged cell phone numbers—though I explained to him my signal fades in and out.

As we neared Jason's driveway, the sergeant flagged me over and we stopped about a quarter mile from the driveway. He told me that he wanted me to wait here, inside the unmarked squad car. The rest of the patrol drove away, out of view and back to the scene of the crime where the shooting took place. After a short while, the sergeant called me.

"We've got Jason's mom here, and she says Jason isn't around and hasn't seen him in two years. She says he's in Florida." I told him about the ticket Jason got only a few miles away just 10 days ago—and that I thought she was lying. The sergeant agreed she was probably lying, noting the speeding ticket he recently got up here. He told me that the shooter was Jason's mom's boyfriend. The boyfriend told police that he didn't recognize me or see my badge and just saw me turn around and leave. He also told the sergeant that after I left, he just went out back and did some target shooting.

"I hate to tell you but we can't do anything about this. We can't get him for shooting his rifle as he's not in city limits and he's on his own property. And we have no witnesses, and so we're gonna have to let him go. We can't prove they are lying in a court of law—as it's just circumstantial evidence."

So, we all headed back into town with our heads hung low. Not because we were disappointed, but because we were afraid to get shot at.

As for Jason, we did later find out that he was on the lamb down in Florida, so it was time to close the case on my end, and pass it down to some lucky bastard P.I. in Florida.

Dart Man

The phone rang exceptionally early on this morning. The attorney was anxious to have two of us come to their office for a meeting. It was a high-profile case that they needed us to work on.

I picked up Gabe and we headed down to their law office. We sat down in the meeting room with the lawyers— and they plopped down a stack of papers taller than my Brandy bottle. The paralegal leaned back in her leather chair and explained to us, "This is a summons and complaint we need you to serve on a local businessman. You might need to do some surveillance and undercover work on this one."

I glanced down and looked at who the defendant was. I couldn't believe it. I pointed it out to Gabe and he just smiled. We've had a past history with this guy.

"Kevin A. Johnson, eh?" I said to her.

"You know him?"

"Oh yeah. He's a real asshole. What's he up to now?"

It turns out he is pals with our coin collector friend, Vincent. Their coin and vending businesses were just fronts for other shady dealings they had going on.

She went on to explain, "Apparently, Kevin and Vincent were making business trips out to Colorado. While they were there, they stayed in fancy hotels and hired 'escorts' for the weekend. It seems Kevin took and liking to one of the escorts and arranged a place for her to stay here locally, and ended up getting married to her. They managed to hide this from their ex-wives for a while—until Kevin's ex-wife found out and lit the fire on this one. Now she is taking legal action against him and filing for divorce, and the escort is also filing a law suit against him for sexual abuse and false imprisonment to name a few. Here, read this article," she said as she tossed a newspaper clipping in front of us.

He told me I had to be a good slave, was the headline.

The story went on to read:

She was forced to call her husband "master." Marilyn O'Brien says she faced a list of 'punishments' if she wasn't naked when he came home.

A 'slavery contract' details those repercussions, as well as a demand that she submit to Kevin's "total dominance and control," she claims.

But after years of alleged physical abuse and sadomasochistic activities, O'Brien says she has had enough.

She's not only divorcing her 50-year-old husband but also has filed a separate lawsuit that accuses him of cheating her on joint business dealings, photographing her bound-and-gagged body, and causing a 'wronging death' by forcing her to abort a child against her will.

It was all part of a lifestyle, she claims, that included sex with high-priced call girls brought to their Gold Coast condo and regular beatings at their Wisconsin house. Her lawsuit includes sexually explicit pictures that her husband allegedly took and she later found.

"He told me I had to be a good slave. He also told me not to tell anybody about any of this, or my face would be beaten so badly, I wouldn't recognize it in the mirror," O'Brien, 45, said in an interview that also included her attorney, Dean Dicker.

Me and Gabe looked at each other. I had to say it, "Dean Dicker? You gotta be kidding me!"

The story continued:

Neither Johnson or his attorney returned calls. But in an affidavit filed in the couple's pending divorce, Johnson says his wife is making it all up.

"I have never been abusive to her," he said.

Court records in Wisconsin show police have arrested Johnson multiple times in domestic violence incidents and that investigators once found O'Brien with bruises and whip marks on her body.

Johnson has one domestic violence-related conviction on his record. It stems from and October 4 incident in which he originally was charged with battery. In March, he pleaded guilty to a lesser charge of disorderly conduct.

O'Brien never actually signed the slavery contract, but she said Johnson verbally enforced it. "I was so scared of him," she said.

The couple met in Aspen, Colorado. He says in his affidavit that he hired her as an escort for the weekend. He kept hiring her, he says, later entering into a five-year relationship and, finally, a five-month marriage.

She denies that she was an escort and says they met by chance, continuing to date as they traveled extensively, starting a coin collecting business together and bought property. Her lawsuit seeks more than $60 million in damages and alleges that Johnson is hiding money from the IRS.

"It was the life styes of the rich and famous," Dicker said. "He sucked her in. Only when you peel back the veneer do things become problematic."

Dr. Laura Berman, a Chicago sex therapist who runs the Berman Center and writes a column for the Chicago Sun Times, said the lifestyle—with willing partners—is more common than most realize.

"These are your neighbors, the parents of kids at your school," she said. "It's not like their freaks."

Gabe nudged me and laughed, "I'd say you're wrong there, Doc—they are definitely freaks!"

The story continued:

O'Brien's story, she said, sounds like she probably signed up for something different than this became. O'Brien says she couldn't believe the change in her husband's behavior.

Johnson, she claims, wields substantial political power in Wisconsin and Minnesota, where he run video gambling companies, among other ventures.

That's why she filed her lawsuit in Cook County Circuit court. I want to do something to see this addressed further.

I'm Not in Here

The Set Up

I opened today's mail and got a new assignment. A new client—some lawyer in Texas needed a guy served up in Easton. I've dealt with Texas lawyers before, and either I didn't get paid, or I got the proverbial Texas longhorn up the backside. This one was going to be a challenge. Apparently, the client had the Sheriff try serving him the court Summons, but they were unable to get the job done. So, it's up to me again, as a professional private investigator to handle the shit jobs they can't.

The Journey

It was a hot August day as I drove to Easton. I found the place easy enough—it turned out to be a house that was turned a duplex. I didn't know if my subject lived upstairs or down, but it didn't matter, as there wasn't anyone home in either one. Another slumlord house— needed paint (badly) and the rickety stairs creaked as I walked back down them. There was no garage and no cars parked outside. In the back there was a spot on the lawn, where it looked like there was once a garage, but perhaps mother nature did us a favor by blowing it away, piece by piece. What was left standing wasn't pretty. I decided to hold out for a while on this one—wanting to try and impress a new client.

There was a boat dealership just down the road—the parking lot there proved to be a good discreet place to sit and wait and see if anyone comes home. I got out my infamous binoculars, and watched the house. Two hours went by before I gave up—*to hell with him, I've got other papers to serve and I need to do something that actually makes money.*

I went back a few days later. *Shit.* No cars parked outside again. So, I went back and parked next to the boats down the road, and waited. Again. This time it paid off. Nearly two hours later someone showed up. A male driver in an old Volkswagen Bug. *Damn. I haven't seen one of those in years. Jesus—it's still one of the ugliest vehicles ever made. No wonder Hitler lost the war. What stupid son of a bitch would design such a contraption and think he could take over the world?*

I got a good look at the driver through the binoculars, and I wasn't too surprised to see he was a tall lumbering idiot. He had to be an idiot to drive this old rusty piece of crap car. He walked towards the stairs and looked like he was lost at his own house. I watched as he walked up the rickety old stairs to his apartment. I drove slowly over there, giving him just enough time to settle in to watch his favorite titty flick and crack open a Pabst Blue Ribbon beer.

As usual, I didn't park right in front of the house. Although I was still in shooting distance, I parked by the neighbor's house and walked up to the ugly old house. As I walked up the stairs, they creaked louder than a group of old whores running a marathon.

I knocked on what was left of the screen door. I didn't want to knock too hard for fear of the damn thing falling off. There was a doorbell, but I didn't want to even touch it as it was hanging off the house by the wires. The wind was banging it against the house so hard I thought maybe it would ring for me.

No such luck. I kept pounding on the door as the idiot wouldn't answer. I knew he was inside. I yelled out, "Lance! Would you come to the door please!"

I was met with silence. Did this guy think I was going to give up that easy? I pounded even harder on the door a second time. I yelled out again, "Lance! I know you're in there! I'm a detective from Wisconsin and I need to talk to you for a second."

"Come on, Lance, I know you're in there and I'm not going anywhere," I said.

I finally got a reply. I heard a voice yell back to me, "I'm not in here!"

"Oh. OK. Is this Lance's ghost I'm talking to? Lance— I saw you come home a few minutes ago, now get out here."

He finally opened the door and I got a closer look at Lance. He smiled, and from that I presumed, this guy has never sat in a dental chair in his whole bum life. Luckily, he didn't put up a fight and took the papers from me. I didn't have to waste any good ammo on him today.

"You need to show up in court on the 30th," I told him. As I walked away, he held the papers with one hand and scratched his ass with the other. I got back to my car, hoping that Lance's 'ghost' could read, because I was pretty sure that Lance could not. I got back to the office OK.

Never did get paid for this one. As a matter of fact, six months later, I had to take those Texas lawyers to court. Maybe you'll see us on Judge Judy.

As the author of this book, over the years, I wanted to do something in the line of detective work to contribute to society in a positive way. For years, I worked for a major corporation, in a department called Plant Engineering. In that time period, I worked part time security at the World Trade Center in St. Paul, Minnesota. As the years went by, I took tests through the state of Minnesota and became a certified gun instructor for the DNR and the State of Minnesota. About two years later, I wanted to make extra money to support my family and brush up on my state and federal laws, so I studied hard and got my Minnesota real estate license. By achieving all the above, it looked good when I applied that information to my detective resume to become a well-rounded detective for the state of Wisconsin. After all those hard years of work, the day came when I had to study hard to know federal and state laws of Wisconsin, in order to pass the test to become a licensed Wisconsin "P.E.," and I achieved that. Hey, not bad for a kid that grew up on ten acres of woods in rural Wisconsin.

Are You Ready to Catch Some Fish?

Part 1

Winter had set in. It was a particularly cold and snowy December. Gabe and I walked into the office for a nice cup of hot coffee (and rum).

Heather, our new secretary, was already there and warming up the place, with just her looks. Her blonde hair and looks were enough to melt the snow and fog up the windows.

"I've got a new assignment for you guys," she said. "I just got off the phone with Walter, and he's got a case for you two up north at Bass Lake. He wants you to call him back."

Walter was one of our oldest clients—an insurance lawyer who wore a bow tie and always smoked a custom-made pipe. We were never sure what he would put in that pipe, but he paid well and on time.

We went to the conference room and called Walter and sat down with our coffee and rum.

"Hi, Walter, this is Steve. I've got you on speaker phone with Gabe here," I told him.

"I've got a big case for you two. I've got this guy up north at Bass Lake. It's a work comp case and he's claiming a bad back and total disability. However, I've got a tip he is working as a fishing guide on the lake. He wants a half million dollars to settle, and I'll be damned if I'm gonna give him one damn dollar. I want you both to go up there and check it out. You have an open check book on this one. I want lots of videotape of this guy and what other information you can get. I'll fax you over the details."

"We'll head up there this weekend," I told him before hanging up. A few minutes later we received his fax.

It would seem that the subject, a certain Jake Adams, hurt his back at work and is now on total disability. We got his home address near Bass Lake, a description of him, his vehicles and everything else we needed to get started.

Heather did her part, and called around up at Bass Lake and managed to get a hold of Mr. Adams. She played her part as a housewife who wanted to surprise her husband with a weekend of fishing and relaxation. Mr. Adams was very open about his talents as a fighting guide, and told her he even has cabins for rent and has one open for this weekend. So, Heather reserved a cabin and we were set.

Our plan was to go up separately. I would stay in the cabin and go out fishing with Mr. Adams, while Gabe would check in at a hotel in town and discretely follow us around while videotaping Mr. Adams. Gabe packed up his gear, including a portable ice fishing tent, camcorders, undercover cameras, and lots of batteries and blank tapes.

The following Friday afternoon, we headed up—not knowing what kind of a wild weekend lay ahead of us.

Part 2

We drove separate cars for the four-hour trip to Bedford, which is located next to the lake. As we drove through town, I notice that this was a typical small American town: I gas station, one small creepy motel, and five bars.

Gabe stopped in at the motel to check in, and I went to one of the bars. While gulping down a few cocktails, I talked with the bartender and got some feedback about the town. I mentioned to him that I was from out of town, and up here on a weekend ice fishing trip away from the wife.

"Where you staying at?" he asked me.

"I'm staying at one of the cabins on Bass lake, and I hired a fishing guide to show me around."

"Oh!" he said back to me. "Are you staying at one of Jake's cabins?"

Looking back at the bartender, I forced a smile and told him, "Yes."

"That's great. He's a good guy. He comes in here just about every night!"

"Well, he's also my fishing guide—so, you might be seeing us come in together."

I left the bar and headed towards my cabin. I found the office—a large house on the lake.

The little bell on the door rang as I walked in. Here I finally met Jake Adams. He was a big guy with a big beard. He seemed very outgoing and pleasant. I almost felt guilty that we were about to nail this guy to the wall—until I remembered that he was a scammer. Jake told me he would come to my cabin at 7 am to pick me up.

I saw a map of the lake on the wall behind him, so I asked him, "Where are we going to start off at?" I told him, pointing at the map.

He pointed to a spot near the middle of the lake, not far from shore. "I've got my ice shacks right here," he said. "So, tomorrow you don't need to bring anything. I've got all the fishing gear, food, and beer ready to go."

After paying him, I went to the cabin to unpack. I called Gabe up to go over our plan for tomorrow.

"Gabe! How's the hotel?"

"It's not hotel happiness!" he told me. "I'm glad I have my gun with me to shoot the rats that run across the floor."

"Yea, I know what you mean. I should have brought a few mouse traps myself. OK. Jake is picking me up at 7:00 tomorrow morning. He's got a red Chevy pickup parked outside his place—so I imagine we'll be in that. I explained to Gabe where he had his ice houses. You'll have to get out there before us and set up your portable ice tent and camcorders."

"OK," Gabe said. "I'm having a few beers and go to bed."

It was such a good idea I did the same.

Part 3

The next morning Jake was right on time, knocking on my cabin door. I was ready to go, so I opened the door and stepped outside.

"Are you ready to catch some fish?"

"Let's go," I said. I was hoping that Gabe was already out there and ready to catch us on film. We got into his Chevy truck and headed down to the lake. There was plowed trails leading to the various ice shacks.

After a few minutes, we arrived at a group of ice houses near the middle of the lake. I was happy to see that Gabe's tent was in our group.

"These four are mine," Jake explained, pointing to the closest ice shacks. I looked over at Gabe's tent and hoped that he remembered to try and keep me out of the picture and get Jake on film by himself.

"The first thing we need to do," Jake continued, while lifting a heavy ice auger out of the back of his truck, "Is to drill some holes out here. We'll put tip-ups on the holes out here and fish inside."

I stood back away while Jake pull-started the gas-powered auger. Once he got it started, he began drilling a hole through the thick ice. He appeared to be putting the full weight of his so-called bad back into it without any problem. I couldn't help but to crack a little smile as I glanced over at Gabe's ice fishing tent. There was a plastic window on the side of his tent facing us, and also the zipper door was slightly open—I didn't know which one Gabe was using to see through, but in either case he was hopefully getting a clear shot of Jake and his auger.

Once he finished drilling through the ice, he lifted the heavy auger out of the ice and walked about ten feet over. "We'll drill about three holes out here," he shouted to me, through the loud noise of the idling auger. "Do you want to drill a hole?" he asked me.

"No, you look like you're having too much fun—you go ahead!" I yelled back. He smiled and began drilling another hole. He effortlessly drilled a third hole, then shut the auger off.

"How many tip-ups do you have?" I asked him.

"I've got five; but we are only allowed to have three set up at one time."

"OK; but can we drill a few more holes, just in case we don't have any luck with these?" I asked.

"Well, I guess so. I might as well do it now while I got the auger out and warmed up," he replied.

He then drilled two more holes in the ice, then put the auger back in his truck. He took out three tip-ups and walked over to the nearest hole. He called me over to show me how to set them up. We put the bait on the end of the fishing line and dropped it down the hole, then pulled back the red flag and set it.

"Once a fish bites down," he explained, "The flag will spring up and we'll know we've got something."

I smiled inside and thought to myself—we've already caught a bigger fish—on film.

"OK, let's go inside," he said to me, after setting up the other tip-ups. We went inside one of his ice shacks and fired up a small wood stove that was in the corner. We cleaned out the slush that was forming in the holes inside and set up a few fishing lines. Jake then went out to his truck and came back with a large heavy cooler. I hoped that Gabe was watching and had the camera rolling.

"That looks pretty heavy—you should have asked for help," I said.

"No, that's OK. I'm pretty fit for my age," he said with a smile.

Jake then grabbed an iron frying pan that was hanging on the wall and set it on the stove.

"I've got everything in here for us," Jake said, opening the cooler. He took out a carton of eggs and a package of bacon, and two beers. He cooked us up a pretty good breakfast, although it was the first time I had beer with my eggs.

We fished for a few hours and had a few more beers.

It was shortly before noon when Jake stood up and said, "I've got a few errands to run. I'll be gone for a few hours—but you should be OK. If you have to piss, you've got the whole lake to relieve yourself on. Oh, and before I go, I'll set up a few lines inside here for you."

After rigging up a few poles, he walked out and left the lake in his truck. I took the opportunity to go out and check in with Gabe.

I went into his tent and saw Gabe sitting on a folding chair and the camera set up on a tri-pod. He had a big smile on his face as he said, "How's the fishing going over there, Steve?"

"Not so good, we haven't gotten anything big enough to catch. How about you—have you caught anything big enough to catch on film?"

"Oh yeah," Gabe said, grinning from ear to ear. "That was great how you got him to dig all those holes outside. I even got him carrying that huge cooler inside."

Gabe couldn't believe me when I told him Jake had cooked me up a great breakfast and brought a lot of beer to drink. "I feel a little guilty about this."

"Why, because he made you breakfast?"

"Well, he also mentioned he was going to cook us up some steak and potatoes for dinner," I said.

"Don't forget—he might be a nice guy but he's a con-artist. As detectives, that's why we are up here."

Suddenly we could hear a commotion in one of the other shacks nearby. We stepped outside and followed the noise of two guys arguing inside a large wooden shack. There were empty beer cans laying everywhere.

"You guys OK in there?" Gabe shouted.

"*No*—help me!" one of the guys yelled back.

Gabe opened the door and saw two large men—one of them sitting on the other and trying to shove his head into one of the holes in the ice.

We rushed in and I grabbed the guy that was on top and pulled him off. They both scrambled to their feet and started arguing again. They were so drunk they could hardly stand up.

We talked with them for a while until they settled down. It turns out they were old friends and fighting over an old girlfriend. They eventually started laughing about it and we decided it was time to get back to work.

Part 4

As we stepped outside, we saw Jake's truck heading towards us from the edge of the frozen lake. Gabe quickly went back in his tent and I returned to my ice shack. I checked the lines for any fish, and luckily found that a fish had hooked on one of them and was just waiting for me to pull it in. I wrestled with it for a minute, and in the process, I backed up and felt my boot hit something. I then heard the 'bloop' sound of something falling in the water. I turned around and looked in the hole behind me and saw the little waves circling in the water as though something had just fallen in.

I scratched my head as I looked around to see if I could tell if anything was missing. I didn't think anything was missing, so I turned my attention back to the fish flopping around on the hook.

I heard Jake's truck pull up and he soon walked into the shack, and saw me wrestling with the fish.

"Woah!" he cried. "You got a good one there. Let me help you get that baby off the hook." Jake took the hook out of the fish and we decided it was a keeper.

"We'll cook that one up with our dinner," he told me.

We sat down and put the fishing line back in the water. After cracking open a few more beers, we started with some small talk. It was about ten minutes later that Jake got up to clean out the holes and check the lines. As he looked into the last hole in the corner, he seemed a little puzzled.

"What the hell happened to my $300 custom fishing rod?" he asked me. A sick feeling came over me as I now realized what I had accidentally kicked into the fishing hole.

"I don't know how to tell you this, but I accidentally kicked it down the hole when I was wrestling with that fish I caught."

He gave me a blank stare for a moment, not knowing what to say. He finally spoke out, "What were you doing, a little all-Star wrestling with a 10-inch fish? How slippery was it?"

"It was so big and slippery I had to body slam that damn fish on the ice," I told him, trying to lighten the mood. Jake didn't see the humor in it—and just continued to stare at me.

"I'm really sorry," I told him. "Look, I'll buy you a new one."

"You buy a new one and add the price onto my bill," I didn't really care, as Walter, my client, would cover the cost. He won't care once he sees all the video Gabe has on Jake and realizes how much money we'll be saving him on this insurance claim.

"Well, OK," Jake said back. "I'll order a new one tomorrow. That'll take care of that."

We fished for a few more hours, caught a few more fish, and soon it was dinner time. Jake cleaned the fish we caught and fried them up with some potatoes.

It was the first time in a while that I saw Jake smile, after we had some fresh fish and a few more beers.

After dinner, it was getting dark and time to pack up and head back. I wanted to let Jake do all the work, carrying all the equipment out to his truck so Gabe could record it all.

"I'd help you carry the heavy stuff out," I told Jake. "But my back's been hurting lately."

"No problem," he said. "I can do this—that's what I'm here for."

After loading up all the fishing gear and coolers and chairs, we headed back to the cabins.

Jake dropped me off and went back to his house. A few hours later, I drove into town and parked in back of the hotel to meet up with Gabe. We checked the video of today's activities and were quite happy with the results. Gabe had caught everything.

"This was a good day, but we I've got tomorrow to go yet," I said. "Are you sure we don't have enough already?"

"Well, we've got an open checkbook on this one, so we might as well enjoy it. Besides, the insurance companies always want us to follow up and see how he's doing the next day, after so much activity."

Gabe agreed, and after a few shots of whiskey we called it a night.

Part 5

The next day was a bright, cool Sunday morning. I had told Jake to pick me up a little later—and so around 10:00 he arrived and we headed back down to the lake.

When we arrived at the ice shacks, I noticed Gabe was already set up nearby. Jake was taking the tip-ups out of the truck and was preparing to set them up.

"Maybe we should drill some holes in a different spot," I told him. "We didn't have much luck yesterday with these."

"Well, OK," he said. "We'll try a few closer to shore."

Once again Jake lifted the heavy auger out of the truck and carried it over to our new spot. Luckily it was still in view of Gabe's blood shot eyes from the night before.

Jake easily drilled a couple more holes and set the tip-ups. We went back inside the shack and fished for a few hours.

"I've got one more thing to show you. But you can't say anything to anyone because it's not legal."

"OK—what do you have in mind?" I asked him, not having a clue as to what he was about to do.

"Follow me," he told me. We stepped outside and walked to an ice fishing tent that was near the shoreline. We went inside and sat down on a bench, near a large opening in the ice where the water was flowing rather quickly.

Jake grabbed a leather carrying case that was under the bench. He opened it up and took out a small ice fishing rod. He then pulled out the bottom of the case to reveal a hidden compartment, where he took out what looked like a fishing spear.

"Have you ever been spear fishing before?"

"No, I haven't. Isn't it illegal?" I asked him.

"Well, it is—but no one's gonna see us out here!"

I thought to myself, I know one person who might: Gabe, my detective partner.

"How do you do it?" I asked. Jake then showed me how we just sit and wait for the fish to come swimming by in the shallow water, then spear them and pull them out. We took turns 'catching' a fish about every five minutes. After we had a good harvest, we put the fish in a pail and headed back to our shack.

Jake cleaned the fish, and cooked them up with a few more potatoes and onions. After our feast, I told Jake I was ready to head back. We had some fish left over, which Jake told me he would package and send home with me.

Once again, Jake loaded all the equipment back into his truck and we soon headed off the lake and back to my cabin. I told Jake I would pack my things up and meet him at his office to pay the bill.

At his office, I paid the bill, which included a new customized fishing rod. Jake also gave me the packaged fish and told me to keep it in my cooler.

"It was great showing you around," Jake said. "If you're not in a hurry to leave town, a bunch of us are going to the Hook Inn Bar for a few brews."

"That sounds like fun. I'll see you there in a while."

I drove back to the motel and again parked in the back. I met briefly with Gabe and told him we were wrapping up the case and going to celebrate at the bar.

Gabe packed up his equipment and headed out of town.

I drove to the bar, and upon entering, I saw Jake sitting around a large table with a group of other locals.

"Hey! There you are! Come on over and join us," Jake yelled to me. I sat in with the crowd, had a few beers, and made some small talk.

After quite a few beers more, another local walked into the bar and joined us.

"Scooter!" Jake yelled. "Come on over!"

Scooter joined the crowd, and Jake, in his drunken state, began to open up. "Steve, welcome to the bad back club!"

I asked him what that was—and he explained that Scooter and a few others had worker's comp claims for a bad back and were collecting paychecks "so we can go fishing." After even a few more beers, Jake told me that their little club was going scuba diving next weekend in Cozumel, Mexico.

"No way!" I said to him. "I've been there before. Where abouts are you going diving?"

Jake took a napkin and proceeded to draw a map of Cozumel and drew exactly where they were going diving offshore. "I'll have to keep this," I said, putting the napkin/map in my pocket.

"Next time I'm there, I'll have to check this out."

The 'bad backers' took turns telling their stories of how they "got injured," and were scamming the insurance companies.

Enjoyed their tales and the local ale, and after a few more drinks, perhaps too many, I headed home.

It was good to be back home, and after bringing all my equipment inside I headed straight for bed.

The next day we met with Walter, our client, and gave him our videotapes and reports. He was quite happy with it all, and paid us our fee with a nice bonus.

"By the way," Walter said to us. "I've got a cabin up north. Would you like to go fishing sometime?"

"No!" we both said at the same time.

"I think I'll get my fish at the grocery store next time," Gabe told him. "We've had enough fishing for a while. I don't want to smell any fish for a long time."

We left Walter's office, hoping that his next assignment for us would not involve sitting on a bucket on a frozen lake catching smelly fish and smelly scammers.

It wouldn't be until the next weekend when I began to smell something very bad inside my house. It was then that I remembered about the fish in the cooler that I had left inside the doorway.

I would never have an appetite for fish again. And, oh yeah, I would never use that cooler again.

Lake Street

1. The Assignment

Just another usual day in the office. A few shots of whiskey for breakfast and we are ready for a day's work. I looked through the pile of mail, and saw a registered letter from some attorney in Minneapolis. I never liked going to Minneapolis—it seems that the city is trying to compete with Chicago for the highest murder rate. It looks like we have to serve an older woman who was scamming others and credit unions out of a lot of money.

2. The Job

I headed out to the big city one Thursday night—you never want to go there without less than two guns hanging on your shoulder. Especially around Lake Street.

As I arrived at dusk, I drove past the house I was looking for, and saw that it was an older mansion style house, built in the World War Two era. There was an old, wooden white 8 foot high fence surrounding the house. I noticed that most of the other houses on the street had barred windows and other fenced in yards. I parked down the street and got the binoculars out to do little surveillance work. I heard the sound of a car approaching at a high speed. I looked down the street and saw the driver holding out a large, oversized McDonald's bag out the window. He locked up his brakes in front of a neighbor's house and gave the bag a heave-ho onto the poor guy's nice green lawn—where it broke apart and spread the Big Mac's garbage all over the front lawn.

Shit. Nice neighborhood.

I sat back in my leather seat and resumed my gaze upon the house in question. Darkness was settling in on the city, and I could now observe lights on in the alley and in back of the house. The house was completely dark, so I assumed Alice was not home. I quietly got out of my Lincoln, gently closing the door and walked up to the back alley where there was a detached garage. I realized that there was a light sensor on her garage that was triggered every time a neighbor or anyone else would drive by. I spotted a neighbor in the alley coming out his side garage door. I walked up to him and asked him about Alice.

He first looked at my badge around my neck and asked "Can I help you?"

"Have you seen Alice around lately?"

"I don't care about Alice, I don't want to see Alice, and let me tell you this—she aint pretty, but she is scarry."

I thanked him for his useless information and let him walk away. I glanced back at Alice's house and saw that it was still completely dark. No cars parked outside and no activity inside. I spoke with another neighbor, and older woman, and she told me that Alice drives an older white

Ford van with Minnesota plates, and that she usually parks on the street. She had little else to offer, so I headed back to my Lincoln.

About an hour later and after still nothing had happened, I decided I had to go to the bathroom—my teeth were floating and I don't even have false teeth. I got out of the car and wanted to stretch out and walked up to a gas station a few blocks away.

As I entered the "gas" station, I noted the bars on the windows and asked the cashier about the bars on the windows. He had one simple answer:

"After dark it can get pretty bad around here."

I asked for the bathroom key, and he handed me the key with a fake plastic hand grenade attached. I looked down at this hand grenade and had an explosive thought, "What in the hell am I doing here?"

I relieved myself in the bathroom of horror, as it looked like it was the last holdout of Bonnie and Clyde.

I walked away from the gas station. I saw a restaurant on the comer and thought I could go in for a sandwich to take with me. I approched the front door, and see lights on inside, but found the front door was locked. There was a lit neon "open" sign in the front window. Suddenly, a large tall black gentleman appeared behind the front door, and after looking me over he unlocked and opened the front door. As I reluctently went inside, I heard him close and lock the door behind me, using all three deadbolts.

As I appraoched the counter, I noticed a rather unappealing woman behind the counter. She asked me what I wanted, and to keep it simple, I told her I wanted a tuna fish sandwich.

As she smiled and said, "Okay!" I observed that she had a wad of tobacco in her mouth and turned around, as if to hide it from me, spit a load into an empty Pabst Blue Ribbon can. "One Tuna Fish Sandwich coming up!"

I was glad to see the sandwich was pre-wrapped. After paying her and making sure to leave a good tip so as to get out safely, I walked back to the front door and had my giant friend unlock the door for me to leave. He turned around looked straight into my eyes and said, "You weren't hitting on my woman, were you?"

I just walked away as he smiled, locking the door behind me.

I returned to my Lincoln, which was luckily still there with no parts missing. As I sat in the front seat, deciding whether or not to bite into this sandwich, I noticed that a white van with Minnesota plates was now parked near Alice's house in the street.

Lights started popping on in various rooms at her house, so I knew that someone was finally home. I got out of the Lincoln with the court Summons in one hand and my fingers on my revolver on the other. I walked up to the house but couldn't see anything over the fence. I noticed a large mound in the neighbor's yard, so I walked over and as I stood on top I could see over Alice's fence, and saw her through an open door as she was holding a small package in the kitchen area. I approached the house and grabbed the front gate of the fence and opened it slightly. Before I could move, a large German Shepard lunged at me, showing his teeth. I quickly slammed the gate shut before he took a bite out of me.

I yelled over the fence, "Alice! I am a Private Detective and have some court papers I have to serve you?"

Alice yelled back, "I don't want any court papers and I'm not coming out there!"

I looked down the fence line and saw a large hole. I walked over and peered through the hole, seeing that Alice had walked out and was close to the fence near me. I rolled up the court summons and made sure the rubber band was tightly around it, then tossed it over the fence, hitting Alice on the shoulders.

I yelled to her, "Alice, you are officially served on behalf of the State of Wisconsin and you better show up in court." As I walked away, I could hear Alice yell back at me over the fence, "You son-of-a-bitch!"

I walked back to the Lincoln, called the agency and let them know the job was done. I started the Lincoln, ready to get out of Alice's Wonderland. I saw an ugly stray dog walk up to my car and started sniffing around. I looked down and smelled the tuna fish sandwich, and thought maybe this dog could use it more than I. So, I unwrapped the tuna sandwich, and tossed it out to the poor dog and drove off. I looked into the rearview mirrow as I left and saw that the dog gave the sandwich one sniff, and shook his head and looked sickly as I drove away.

This is detective Gabe G Kemling after a hard day's work having my favorite watermelon spiked with top-shelf whiskey.